THE DESTRUCTION OF TIME

The Destruction of Time

Copyright © 2021 by Thomas G. Morgan. All rights reserved.

Cover: Jimmy Smith at an unknown location from Laurie & Cuscuna
"Blue Note Story" photo: Francis Wolf

Published by Mindstir Media, LLC

45 Lafayette Rd | Suite 181| North Hampton, NH 03862 | USA

1.800.767.0531 | www.mindstirmedia.com

Printed in the United States of America

ISBN-13: 978-1-7363845-7-2

THE DESTRUCTION OF TIME

THOMAS G. MORGAN

MINDSTIR MEDIA

For my sons;

Eliot Thomas

Michael X

Zachary

and Tanner

"He (Malcolm)…became
much more than there was time
for him to be."

Robert Hayden
El Haj Malik El Shabazz

"Time is destitute because it lacks the unconcealedness of the nature of pain, death,
and love. Nature…grants none special cover."

Martin Heidegger
What Are Poets For?

"Time is what keeps the light from reaching us.
There is no greater obstacle to God than time."

Meister Eckhart
The Complete Mystical Works

"Time is…not."

Ezra Pound
The Pisan Cantos

Table of Contents

Shatteredness ◄──────► Scatteredness
Scatteredness ◄──────► Shatteredness

The Dialectique of Destruction

When what's happenin

is happenin too damn fast

souls scatter <----> time shatters

into miniscule comets that keep

causing your coffee to get cold

Time,

that metrical[1] measure

imposed upon Being, whose falleness

roils between the bloodshed of birth and death

A test so terminal if so ordered with

Scattered shackles of quantified time

can blind, pervert and isolate

standpoints toward the immeasurable

clear moment temporally indeterminate

"Concernfully encountering"[2] this olde world to dwell

autonomously[3] recused from unjust utility.

Recusant to times manipulation is to dwell

as of now and of yore…poetically

[1]Music is sound taking charge of time
taking charge of sound

[2]Martin Heidegger (Sein Und Zeit)

[3]David Riesman (Lonely Crowd)

Having been there is "futural"[4]
To 'being there' past present horizons
febrile rot and fragmentation
As God wills to detonate the present.

When concern fades to fear
it falls for "a jumble
of hovering possibilities"[5]
no hold on any definite…possibility

Entanglement ensues…
"which precludes allegiance
when what has been surmised gets carried out!"[6]
…(in deed, the opportunity to keep on surmising is snatched away.)

Torn back from snatch to ambiguity…
then swamped in surmising others' intents
and purposes to how we feel about it.
Comportment and reply in a pig's eye

Trustworthy ancients prophesy
flaking equations
in quaking gradations
is heard our non-dehiscent cry.

[4]Martin Heidegger (Sein Und Zeit)
[5]IBID
[6]IBID

Michael McNaughton & TGM iin Morelos at Christian - Marxist Seminar

PREFACE

In 1960, Tom hitch hiked throughout Western Europe, spending the winter in fascist Spain and reaching Moscow for May Day in 1961. Returning to Indiana he chaired the student faculty committee at ISU that founded the Eugene V. Debs Foundation for Socialist History and Thought. Working with the Wabash Valley Labor Council and (CORE) the 'Congress for Racial Equality' significant desegregation was achieved in Terre Haute. By May 1, 1962, he was indicted with Ralph Levitt and Jim Bingham, co-defendant officers of IU's Young Socialist Alliance. They were charged with conspiring to overthrow the government. They faced two to six years imprisonment from Indiana's 1952 McCarthyite anti-subversive laws, which illegalized two or more persons meeting to discuss "unamerican" Marxist ideas. The Y.S.A. defended the Cuban Revolution, advocating self-defense for black communities afflicted by racist violence, opposed the war in Vietnam, and were further accused by the prosecutor of "a running gun battle with the state of Kentucky". (We'd "run" canned goods to families of the striking U.M.W. coal miners in Harlan, KY... and been shot at.. The 'Bloomington Three' young revolutionaries traveled extensively throughout the US and Canada for their International Defense Committee chaired by Bertrand Russell. Tom read his poetry and spoke at platforms in 32 states. I traveled with him through much of the deep south where our Indiana license plates provoked steady hostility from the police. Yet we were consistently received by diverse groups of people with great hospitality and Tom's poetry while sometimes wildly abstract seemed to always connect with his listeners whether they were academics or share croppers. His verse and voice was a resonant call for justice; "by God almighty" the collective response.

I would comradely appeal the reader treat Tom's poems with respect for the challenge they present. Tread seriously as through an incomprehensible mine field toward the safety and wisdom of what Heidegger calls the fundamental language of being; the poetic. The reward here is real poetry from a true poets mind crafted verse. The best remind me of my experience studying an assigned poem in 1960 Germany. It was called 'Die Nact' by Walther Von Dervogelwide and seemed as difficult to get through as it was to pronounce the poets name. From my austere seminary room on the left bank of the Neckar in Heidelberg to Brechtian performances in East Berlin and the more affluent digs Tom and I acquired on Lake Wahnsee...I pondered that poem. Then late one night while reading aloud it became resonant with as they say a voltage flow of maximum amplitude. I got it!...in ways that only poetry can discharge. Getting it with the poetry of Thomas G. Morgan is to amply wrestle those many angels concurrent and convergent to time, place, and the liminal grail of his muse. Intellectually proletarian, aesthetically pastoral he argues unyieldingly the finer points of critical inclusion without compromise or condemnation. Not judgmental he is nonetheless consistently partisan testing validities. 'Olde Bloody Toms'* new verse like his old life (he's claimed to be pushing 80 for several years now and his suggestion in 'Shotgun Preacher' that "the secret of aging well is to get old early") affirms conservative traditional values and revolutionary socialist politics. A wondrous contradiction demonstrable in his faithful loving solidarity for family, friends and comrades under the ancient code of Gods authority ordering careful relations and boundaries of behavior for collective human justice, husbandry of other creatures, and stewardship for the land. He cares for 20-25 pysc. patients a week (partisan to their working class injuries and struggles vs government and corporate agencies), farms with a team of mules, tends a flock of 100 sheep and goats, 7 broodmares and stands a champion trotter at public stud. All – with the radically continuing substantiveness of hard work. Significant? I think so…A diligent and healing sign for our ailing times! Mike McNaughton: Founder of Indiana's Fair Play for Cuba Committee. (May 1, 2019)

* "Olde Bloody Tom" – family nick name.

POPE FRANCIS   FIDEL

A requiem mass was said for Mike at St. Josephs in Terre Haute and Rockville July 30, 2019.
Just as requiem mass was said for Fidel at St. Josephs 3 years earlier November 27, 2016;
that these comrades for socialist justice have eternal rest in peace.

INTRODUCTION

From the spring of 1962 to the fall of 1965 my co-defendants Jim Bingham, Ralph Levitt and I were "on tour" for CABS, Committee to Aid the Bloomington Students. We were surprised and grateful for the grass roots support we received. AFL-CIO organized labor, the American Association of University Professors, Jewish Temples, Christian Churches, Islamic Mosques, rank and file diligence of the Socialist Workers Party, solidarity support from the Communist Party USA and Y.P.S.L of the Socialist Party.

However we were especially appreciative of the Black Communities support for us. For it was more than political. There was an important spiritual dimension to it. Black men, women, and children assembled regularly in their churches, mosques, and meetings with a concentrated power of coordinated passion and moral solidarity for justice. No wonder Lenin thought American Revolution required informed and organized black communities.[7] Or as W.E.B. DuBois would say; the "Souls of Black Folk." Representative leaders of these souls were many but, we were especially grateful for Rev. Martin Luther King and Malcolm X. The dialectic between Martin's determined gentleness and Malcolm's unrelenting militancy leveraged the rise of a fierce consciousness that defeated the war makers in Vietnam and smashed segregation in America.

Similarly we are thankful for those sounds of the last century that inspired us to struggle on for justice, celebrate our achievements and endure our losses. That is, "the music" … that splendid Jazz and all those splendid jazz musicians[8] best exemplified by the archetypal dialectic between players like John Coltrane and Miles Davis. Between Tranes' muscular compassion in 'A Love Supreme' interpenetrated by the dangerously cool menace of Miles in 'Elevator to the Gallows'. ("Ascensur pour l'chefaud") Those rubatoesque[9] sounds arranged and improvised our stolen time!

Hard times gave us hard bop thoughts and cool resistance to co-option. No moral rela-

---

[7]"The struggle against racism is central to the revolutionary process in America".
V.I. Lenin's speech to the second congress of the Third International, 1926

[8]all those splendid jazz musicians. To name but the most of many who brought in our stolen time; there was Coleman Hawkins, Roy Eldridge, Red Norvo, Thelonius Monk, Charley Bird Parker, Max Roach, Dizzy Gillespie, McCoy Tyner, Duke Ellington, Count Basie, Bud Powell, Henry Clark, Chet Baker, Gerry Mulligan, John Lewis, Milt Jackson, J.J. Johnson, Ahmed Jamal, Yuseef Lateef, Frank Morgan, Lee Morgan, Red Garland, Sonny Rollins, Jimmy Rushing, Jimmy Cobb, Shadow Wilson, Sarah Vaughn, Billie Holiday , Buck Clayton, Buddy Rich, Flip Phillips, Todd Damerson, Ella Fitzgerald, Horace Silver, Jimmy Smith, Art Blakey, Clifford Brown, Elvin Jones, Philly Joe Jones, Idris Muhammed, Duke Pearson, Wayne Shorter, Sam Rivers, Ornette Coleman, Herbie Hancock, Tony Williams, Ike Quebec, Blue Mitchell, Bobby Hutcherson, Bennie Green, Chico Hamilton, Chick Corea, Stan Getz, Dave Brubeck — hey, I even dug Paul Desmond; jazzmen not responsible for racist marketing

[9]rubato: adj. adv. [tempo rubato, stolen time] Music defying a conventionally strict tempo

tivism.[10] We were dogmatically[11] principled as is required in music according to Igor Stravinsky no less than in politics. Stravinsky further notes in his 'Poetics of Music', "that the words dogma and dogmatic however sparingly one may apply them to aesthetic matters or even to spiritual matters never fail to offend – even to shock – certain mentalities richer in sincerity than they are strong in certitudes." He quotes Remy de Gourmont saying, "Sincerity then is hardly an explanation and is never an excuse."

Miles Davis and John Coltrane led on dogmatically certain as Malcolm and Martin with sounds of being way out there beyond bop with long periods on one chord not losing modal velocity yet without any nervous ass need to get there fast. Even when playing ostinato gatling gun fast they managed to never sound in a hurry. Beside, behind, on top of the note or inferring past it they were cool, calm and collected. They took their time as we might seize ours. Destroying its shackles, overcoming those times toward a different level of consciousness, one that is distinct from all fostered time. Revolutionary advancing and dogmatically solid like Chestertons[12] concurrently restorative curve. No nihilistic noise or rant but "beauty earned through strife and toil."[13] They left time keeping to those who cared about it. Drummers Tony Williams and Elvin Jones with McCoy Tyner on the key board so polyrhythmically reorganized for Tranes "reharmonizations" that a collective ability to shift time itself was developed. They got after the three tonic approach like Tesla after space craft; arrayed with greater sounds and discovered dissonance than ever heard before …"Countdown" "Kind of Blue" "Milestones" "But not for me" "26-2." No going back to entertainment! These were sounds to ponder.

To think through deeply, carefully considering life's wide range of connective experiences. Music set to montage your inner vision. Relations of the soul. For "Universally, relations stop nowhere, and the exquisite problem of the artist is eternally but to draw, by a geometry of his own, the circle in which they shall happily appear to do so."[14]

I was born and lived my first five years at 459 Seventeenth Street in Terre Haute. Down the street and east a block was Claude Thornhill's home. His mom still lived there. We'd see her sometimes when we'd (Dad and me) walk our ponies over to the blacksmith farriers cata corner to her house. She was on Dad's milk route in the later forties and fifties. She was an older lady Mom and Dad would drive places. Dad would always talk about the Claude Thornhill Band. "It was more like an orchestra", he'd say. "The Terre

---

[10]I have written before of how conflict in the 60's was mainly between Liberals and Leftists i.e. moderate moral relativists and radical activists. Confused conservatives wished to conserve injustice and those that didn't still sat out the most American experience of the century i.e. the victory against segregation. Later liberals would claim credit for the movement they missed with the ones they invented i.e. the many so-called sexual liberations.

[11]Poetics of Music by Igor Stravinsky, "we cannot observe a creative phenomena independent of its form. And every formal process proceeds from a principle, the study of which requires precisely what we call dogma".

[12]G.K. Chesterton: "revolution is motion that curves ahead returning toward the point where it started."

[13]Griffin and Washington: "Clawing at the Limits of Cool: definitive history of modern jazz especially its "greatest collaboration" — Miles Davis and John Coltrane.

[14]Henry James

Haute Tribune described its sound as soft as a Wabash Valley Evening".

Jazz historians Griffin and Washington[15] review that aside from Duke Ellington's, Claude Thornhill's was America's most innovative orchestra "utilizing different instruments (including French horns) favoring a dark, subtle, mellower sound than was standard for the big bands." Due largely to its arranger Gil Evans.

Miles Davis, the great improviser, loved arrangers and skilled arrangements; he improvised within them, not without them. He expanded his combo by adding three "arrangers" as sidemen, John Lewis (later of the MJQ), Gerry Mulligan, and Gil Evans from the Thornhill Band. This latter was seismic. Evans brilliantly arranged the most famously effective pieces for Miles then later for John Coltrane and Miles. Birth of the Cool in 1954, Round about Midnight 1955, 'Workin' 1956, At Newport 1958, Giant Step 1959, Kind of Blue 1959, Sketches of Spain 1959, In Stockholm 1960, and the final Miles Davis and John Coltrane: The Complete Columbia Recordings 1961.

This discography of sound we carried in our hearts and minds throughout the next decade. Their new pedal points of pivotal tone seemed to defy finite duration subverting singular reformist expectations. Justice from the courts not to be expected without demonstrable pressure from the streets. Revolutionary destruction of passively attaining justice without losing its militant desire and spirit. Coltrane's sheets of sound seemed visual not only to him but to his listeners. Earthly duration no longer a bum wrap but a nearness to infinity – to God's grace gittin' you there.

That is, if you had the seventh trumpet courage of Miles and his laser beam horn to pierce the uncertainties. Evan's arranged Trane's spiritual quest for God protected by the 'take no shit' from the Devil menace of Miles. Arrangements of "Quiet Fire" Miles called them : announcing a new generation to reject political moderation, nonviolence, and selfies propaganda. Amiri Baraka (Leroi Jones) described them as "Malcolm in the new Super bop fire." And described Malcolm's public speaking; his timing and cadence strikingly like jazz.

Miles long silences and ethereal stretching of time, then Tranes aggressive assault on it puts time away. As in the flamenco "Sketches of Spain". No melody. No set form, but a series of five tonalities behind a one brush pulse marked by drummer Jimmy Cobb quietly – quietly arranged by Evans toward imaging timelessness! Similar to Thelonius Monk's "Straight, No Chaser" but more straight with multi modal chasers.

Lack of harmonic cycles, no progress of clocks with concurrent returns to tone in the mode issued a feeling of timelessness. Miles trumpet flying over the open sea waves of Tranes saxophone. Modal, not exactly measurable. No clock out there. But an unforgotten sense of place.

Both their grandfathers had experienced the evils of racist slavery but also the hard won 14 year freedom and racial democracy of Reconstruction. Before the occupying fed-

---

[15]Farah Jasmine Griffin and Salem Washington 'Clawing at the Limits of Cool'

eral troops left the defeated Confederacy in 1877, prosperous black fathers and mothers had gained their own land with large families and sustainable income to provide for them. All of which was immediately mob ruled away from them. Militancy against oppression is significantly increased when preceded by an arc of success and hope shattered once again. We'll see the same thing as Millennials continue to experience the 21st century decline of 20th century promise and dreams: every kid with a set of permanently loving parents with homes safe from sinful disease blessed by hard work, high wages and no shortage or excess of dollars, affordable access to medical care, education, employment and housing. Like Gene Debs wedding homilies and my mother's mental picture of Heaven; "It'll be a lot like central supply at Union Hospital (where she worked for decades); it will be very clean and everyone will have a job." — My people, America's midwestern working class spoke in tones you could hear on the radio.[16] I explain to my children and grandchildren, "the Amish aren't different from us – they're more like we used to be."

As a midwestern teenaged trumpet player, I listened to recordings of Harry James, Ray Anthony, and Bix Beiderbecke; too coastal! (NY or LA) for me. Satchmo and Al Hirt sounded too southern and Dixielanded. Local players Warren Barbour and Todd Sappington sounded right on. The Miles Davis sound was no coastal and definitely not south land. Downbeat magazine described his tone as very much his own thing but more associated with the Kansas City or Midwestern Sounds. In his autobiography Miles himself says, "That kind of sound in music, that blues, church, back road funk kind of . . . midwestern rural sound…started getting into my blood at six or seven visiting my grandfather's farm. So when I started taking music lessons I might have already had some idea of what I wanted my music to sound like."[17] His cultural landscape held not just the suffering of slavery but also the comeback of Reconstruction that by God no one was going to take away again!

Midwesterners militant long term (long toned) patient persistent perseverance. Close to what the Holy Koran terms "Sabr". Sabr . . sabr that ancient Arabic term implies more meaning than is possible in one English word. Commentary in the Koran notes 5 components. (1) patient non hurried thoroughness (2) perseverance, constancy, steadfast clear purpose (3) disciplined as opposed to spasmodic chancy action (4) cheerful resignation and understanding in sorrow, defeat, or suffering as opposed to murmuring or rebellious whining but saved from mere passivity by steadfast self-restraint from fear, anger, and desire. Hey, that fits Miles whose tone and range stays grounded strong in the middle registries, restrained from technical and/or loud flashiness.

[16]20th Century radio chose the clipped yet easy going accent and tone of the heart landed middle west to represent America's voice to the world.

[17]Miles: The Autobiography (NY Simon & Schuster, 1989

Revolutionary poise; stewardship[18]
apocalyptic and refluent[19]
Soulforce[20] and sabr coalesce
barricades back to the lands care
Bardic prep for the Parthian shot.[21]
We are being roused once again like those ancients in the cave[22] to test our perception
of time and truth beyond our own internal experience. And that in such matters disputes
are unseemly. Better to more sensitively see the bigger picture as Miles understood Isra-
el. "The Arabs and the Jews get along fine; it's the government that's fucked up".

In Sura 18:18 English commentary of the Holy Koran notes "relative fallicious im-
pressions of Time gives us an inkling of the state when there will be no Time, of the Res-
urrection when all our little impressions will be corrected by the Final Reality.

Reverence then for this natural law and Revolution against its abuse becomes the oeu-
vre, the very poetics of our political theology.

T.G.M.

[18]Stewardship: In Laudato si' (papal encyclical on the environment): Pope Francis charges humanity with the stew-
ardship, care and respect for the earth and all of its living creatures by righting the modern capitalist misconception of
"dominion" in Genesis. Indeed. each being is never a mere means for wanton exploitive use. The human person stands
out as created in God's image and evolutionary processes cannot account for the unique irreplaceable dignity each
has as eternally called by God. With this dignity came enormous responsibilities to protect, preserve, and care for the
natural world.

> The Pope would re-enchant this disenchanted world with a grand metaphor of St. Francis. We are to experience
> all natural beings as our brothers and sisters. And this faith-filled poetry is not a pure fantasy because science
> continues to unveil the intricacy, radical connectedness and interdependence of all natural beings… including
> ourselves.
>
> James Hart - Dept. of Religious Studies- Indiana University

[19]Refluent: ebbing as the tide to the sea.

[20]Soulforce: Andrew Young's description of the spiritual power organized by John Lewis in the sixties before he
became a congressman.

[21]Parthian Shot: (a cavalry term) shot at the enemy while retreating or pretending to retreat.

[22]Cave: Gibbon's 'Decline & Fall of the Roman Empire (Ch. 33)" reports a common story from ancient times re: Seven
Christian youths who hid in a cave away from Emperor Decius (240-250 BCE reign) persecution and slept for some
200 years to awake in the reign of Emperor Theodosius II (408-450 A.D.) when Christians religion had become the
state religion. Their perceptions and knowledge remained at that point of time when they had entered the cave.

> The Holy Koran recapitulates that story as an inspired parable where experience, trauma, and memory influence
> individuals to differ in their perception of time and certain facts. And that even with the most honest enquiry
> individuals might reach different subjective conclusions. Better to not indulge this vain sport of time with futile
> details of controversy. Better to keep at work with the tasks of life; beseeching as they did the guidance of Yah-
> weh-Jehovah-Allah for objective clarity and peace.

Death of the cool

(Introit) Every age has its music. A native sound
conceived in the collective soul
of its thematic energies.
Yet no sooner recognized
as the soundtrack of an epoch
it begins to solitarily cease to exist.

After the jazz age
whose tragic promise was captured by Fitzgerald,
depression and war swung american sound around
hot and hip deep into be-bop celebrations
of prosperity. Except, that is

for a single high notes perspective
played throughout manic and minor keyed nights…
brave, and blue, and cool;
cool to mortalities angst.
"Stay cool brothers…
Stay cool" were the last words of Malcolm
and they characterized this sound, style, and time.
The time is past, yet looms
long in the memory of those
who have known and loved it.
Indeed such moments have spared
times ravaging vain fire.

epochal blues

The hounds of night
had bayed
and we heard them despite…despite…

Who started it?
I first heard it
through Miles.
There was Coltrane and the M.J.Q.
Too--------
Old Jazzmen I loved
parlayed performances
These guys and Miles
played right inside my head

We would kill the century
and we could hear it
within our own
interiority…

Recalling the sounds

as you stepped out on Lennox Ave.

…or judged jackstock across the Ohio

in Louisville

You became an agent

of that very sound

dialectique – both within and without

Others could hear you

coming…

too…! Morgan Grey as cockfighter

from Cork to Harlem and the San Joaquin

Thee is back from Berlin

without exactly being

there—

was a coursing of the sound

both hare and hound

in field and spectral sea

Down hundreds of hoosier roads

dunn as the dust

lays easily in August…

As easy as the summer's song

lays easily

upon the dusty foliage.

The sound in your shirtsleeves

driving fast

with the windows down

in hot light

combusting hard and fast

upon a horse

that's humid cool

in heavy covert

The hounds of night

had bayed

…and we'd heard them

despite…

epochal dissonance…

dissonant

expectations

Some other, some others

still might;

'round the century's flickering

pilot…it man

light…

Within…it

and without

Within and without!

postscript set

I recall a reunion…
in the sun of late summer
somewhere in my second decade
I realized all that I loved
was slipping away or…under siege
from insidious foes I could not fathom.
My grandfather Abe – an American improvement
upon seventeen centuries of seriousness
His terrible dignity reigned from where he sat or stood;
a bottle opener by the Pepsis on ice
became a mitre in his hands
My grandmother Katey…who'd died
was still twelve centuries in our mind
her sainted gaze knew the child who'd lied
She was—
and is our weathered purity
Hun poets could not think otherwise
Nor Carlysle…who'd
recognize the trace.
These folk dwelled within their dream
Patriarchal, Pastoral, and Proletarian
Their industry was agri CULTURAL
Against old cancers rage. Yeah.

WHITE NEGROS

We read Norman Mailers 'White Negros' in the fifties. We became white negros in the sixties. And when black people quit being negros we were still stuck with it.

Wary of white racists we bristle for a fight whenever they cross into the ghetto of our consciousness. Hoods of lost context we haunt the periphery of post modern political in correctness.

A glimpse of Julian Bond, a picture of Stokely, a memory of Bob Moses sustains our words as Malcom spoke in the brave contradictions of Dr. King as right on as a Robert Williams rifle club and radio cast from Revolutionary Cuba[23], we recall Ray Charles in those Friday night sounds from the steel mill towards a future out in the street becoming home we would overcome and overthrow all those powers we still put up with…segregating our souls.

[23]Robert Williams, an American refugee from North Carolina broadcast 'Radio Free Dixie' from Revolutionary Cuba into the segregated south.

time is not
Ezra Pound "Time is . . .not" "The Pisan Cantos"

"Time is not" nor the idea that "conversation
should not utterly wither"
your only brave discovery for us
from under the rain minted tent flaps
of political imprisonment
You saw the pale ox
and the white wings of time
compose dark sheep in the drill field
drovered on to mountain clouds
under the guard roosts
God not cluttering the market
nor the masques of perception
for gunneries.
As gunmen tread on your dreams
you wrote with that voltage
that Padraic Colum lost
that we all lost…
in forgotten regiments
in lost legions.

We lost in just cause
"and the mortal fatigue of action postponed"
in "dire crusade"* as Tom Hardy said
because we just couldn't stand as the paraclete stands
in the cusp of the moon.
Plain ground preceding the color
of permanent battle
drawn swords like dark petals of iron
raked like progress into Levitt's tribal obsessions
and Bingham's high Episcopal vagaries.
Codefendants become conspirators for Christ
and the parietals of gender warfare.
John Lewis has lost his lead
for another Sherman's March to the Sea
and Minster Farrakhan has marched
on Washington with a million men
and still left the government standing.
All fallen comrades guard thy rest
Paraclete forever be thy guest.
Feminist members of the Sinn Fein
purge irishmen while the orange reform
for more of their eternal and mindless bullying.

[*dire crusade" from "Souls of the Slain" by Thomas Hardy]

Oh, to be in England now that the Tories are out!

Now that there's room for clout

And the bank is still not the nations

and the long years of patience

And Labour leaders vacillations

Tony and Bill and Evan Bayh and bye are buggering

the right's bottom line

and the left's private parts.

Like your Roehm brothers Berliner das bankgeschaft

aboard the Wabash Cannonball!

We may be bunny rabbit great Wilson ways apart

but How is it far?; if you can think about it.

"Counting sheep in Phoenicia"

or setting tables down by olde rivers

calm as the streams edge lost in the grass

near a breeze by the mute and trumpeting swans

Time is not, yet who are you anyhow?

Is asked in the tules

east of the San Joaquin marshes

and the diablo range

Do you know who you are?

Who in the hell in Indiana are you?

Illusive Americana be who I wanna be

corrected by predestined grace of what I'm gonna be.

It is not far; if you think about it.

Ezra imprisoned in Pisan

poetically dwelling near the Paraclete

standing in the cusp

of the moon.

only by sufferance

"A man's time is his own only by sufferance. There are many ways in
which he may be dispossessed; flood, famine, war, marriage betrayed – not to speak of
death which is the most satisfactory of all because it closes the question finally." Fer-
de-Lance)

When Objibiway hear the owl cry
they know
when it cries for them.

I've heard the owl three times this year
but I'm no Objibiway
my tribal instincts more remote
and consciousness has erased detail

"It is written…"
yet corridors of the atavist
contour around synapses
suggest it nonetheless.

If "it is written" by Allah,
will engages prayer
that He alone may revise
as He wills it anyhow.

From the woods across the road
the owl has cried three times
and whether I've known or not known
and/or Allah revised
I have survived (inshallah)
cancer, pneumonia and heart attack.
The owl cried in October of cancer
and my plumbing ran like rivers backwards
all damned up by the thing.
I explained to red-haired oncologists

who insisted their names were DuGań instead of Dugan
that my family all died of the same thing – TX! (treatment)
and opted against the knife and radiation
not yet ready for Pampers or impotence
I megadosed on herbal remedies
and beat the thing by May.
Would've felt like Solzenietzen
'cept my immunities way down in December
got spiraceted down further with pneumonia
and I almost croaked ruining your Christmas.
We'd talk late about your wanting a life with me
and how I seemed more concerned with death and dying well.
I tried to explain I did not want to die
but if dying, I wanted to do it well.

I had not done it before. It required thought and attention.
"That lonesome valley" "you got to walk . . . . it by yourself"
is lonely precisely because so many others and much of ourselves
want to be somewhere else.
Last week a heart attack anvil fell out of my future,

bombed into my chest, wrenched round my jaw

and half-nelsoned my left arm and ventricle into intensive care.

At the E.R. gate I conspired with a physician bro from Damascus, "Even the Bathists,"

I implored, "have better insurance."

He was game to spring me early 'til the enzymes report

had to be handed on to a Hindu named Desai.

Sweet and serious physician; a Ghandiji

for the warring factions of my heart.

Intensive care indignities;

pissing up a rope, defecating uphill,

poked and probed, dripleashed, and nitro concussioned

with druggy respites for worse . .

the interminable, the infernal TV!

If TV had been on the Titanic

no one would have died on deck

but separately silly and subjectively denying drowning

in their own foster heads.

I watched over 100 hours of CNN and the Starr Report.

William Jefferson Clinton is the most representative President in history.

His bottom line fiscal conservative cowardice

and sexual revolution prowess

truly represents the hearts and minds of the vast majority of his countrymen.

Even his enemies are afraid to impeach him?!

It is time to Impeach the Electorate!

Stand Buchanan on his head and open the borders.

Mexicans, Pakistanis, Africans, Latinos, Hindus too

and Middle Easterners move in and displace this rot.

Anglo Saxon Protestants have had their day and Gog Magoged us up

from their diseased blankets to the indigenous and

their sub-humanizing slavery up to their evangelicanized

idolatry of the self and/or the Presidential penis.

Enough! By God enough!!

It is uncharitable to await their self-destruction.

Some active assistance will help all souls

who scared them after the potato famine

but became dumb and white and moderately modernistically priest-ridden

for the second scare of Southeastern Europe sailing by the Gray Lady

all conscripted democratically with home-grown hicks

to save the British empire for the New World WASPs.

We scared them even more in the sixties.

We restored Reconstruction

and threatened that the bills from the War of the Rebellion

and the Great Depression were consolidated and now due!

We'd become the Dunne boys out to collect.

Out to collectivize the best secular myths

with sacral power to desacralize their lies.

Wars stopped, cruelties halted, and

a brave smile appeared; there was hope throughout the land

and consternation amongst the ASPS

slithering in from country club lawns

with royal memories of the opium war.

They hiss and slide up the arms

of those who might love and lead and labor most.

Drugs and degenerate sex abound

and a new form of idiots call it revolutionary.

Assassinations abound; some publicized, some not

the royal rot was back in force

while hippies humped the air and bikers broke the neck

of black youth in front of the liberated herd of geldings at Altamount.

Hair will not replace thought forever

but brains, blues, and gender were changed forever.

The herd hormonally failed.

Only by sufferance

are the men of the sixties

becoming sixty.

No dialectique, nor trotskyesque mystery,

but the weight of days and dumb numbers

burn them up

and bring them down

…down to the ground.

Decanted from their souls

to this fin de siecle

their critical temperature

a decalescence…

for the time that cools.

Self-styled destinados

buffalo soldiers before their time was done

with their hope and their battle

and their cause on the run.

How desolate these brave

and happy cowboys;

the last breed of this millennium

who could keep their women happy

if not at home!

(postcript set)

Hey…during Mother's last year

'til her death bed

"I'm not sick,…just tired,"

she'd said

Life's force less within her

but hovering about

in some other, kinder ambiance

In earlier times she replied

to my doctrinaire comrades

"You can't bleeve when we die
we're just dead…dead like a dog?
You'll not get off that easy!"
Then she'd describe heaven
as she expected to find it
as a post graduate from purgatory.
"It'll be like central supply
(where she worked at Union Hospital)
…very clean! and everyone will have a job!"
O.K. Wrap it up.
We could use more bass and drums
What about some vibes for rhythm?
How?
It has to be in the reader's head
Postscriptive blues…kebang!
Like terminal Che. In terminal Che.
After meeting for a few moments
Che and his gusano CIA interrogators' conversation
was interrupted by shots!

…followed…by the sounds

of a body falling to the floor…

next door!

"It is better like this Felix, said Che…

I should never have been captured alive this way."

Most of their decalogued recall

runs out a footnote of Reconstruction

and the Great Depression. Noir limits of the thirties. Sounds of the forties

loud outside past post-war presumptions

that were the fifties penetrating pivotally

into that engine of humidities

the fading coals…incendiaries

the men of the sixties.

Humid enough to make the cold war hot

telling it like it is

and was not!

blue not

Trafficked in thinking
is so much jazz
Nightshouldered shots in the dark
discordant about who thought what
and when

Whaddaya expect?
…a silver thread sounding
one clean flute
through it all…
and then

To play it
…to play it,
yet again

swans

Wild swans were with us last year
on cool aquifer waters in warm days they came
to my family estate
swans of the afterlife
beyond the graves
where my parents were lain
leaving us worse than intestate
they died but months separate
serene and at strange angles
to the peace I thought not entirely
passeth my understanding.
The flumes 'round my father twisting
his expression in death as in life
from the darkness overspreading
but for the swans who visited us then
and we look for them this year
we look for them…
again.

green on the ground

Green leaves are falling
cause the drought has leveraged autumn
cold clouds clasp the morning pond
and caress the god damned cockleburs

Dawn's gunfire wound the geese
that fly from the 'nuisance' season
and my neighbors ditch back to covert
by four acres of water close to my heart

Pumping life and pummeled death
is the order of things…my
old gamecock, Zorro, is found dead
near the corpse of a young cockerel contender

Their bloodsport may have excited
my hound pack to take the life
of a ewe I found in the horseweeds
All hounds were sold and I miss their canine company

Combined and uneven is the development
of time around discernment of my father's
presence, his calm ghost and photograph in Labor Day's paper
standing tall and flat-capped near the stamping mill

Supporting 'The General Strike', which ruined
the town, framed far too much of my fate
from the people's finest hour degenerative
the failure of our collective consciousness

The madness of my sibling
I commit to no bad thoughts or feeling
and revere my father's serious fix
on the racing season

I hear his voice in hoofbeats
the way horses speak driving the sound
without sound requiring effort
from senses; perceived from the beloved
Interpenetrating work and value
lives that were lost, in love are found
Life's consciousness like seasons overlie
green leaves upon our ground

The Station of Abraham

Pastures which rivers run beneath
becalm the station of Abraham;
taking his ease
by the sheep pens
at the Pavillion.
Studying…
the seed of his Sovereigns work,
he muses.
He muses on what a long talk they'd had;
the three of them…
codefendants against the Great Accuser
they would conspire
for hours upon criterion
not for hire nor to abuse her
but for permission to go on
They were relaxed and talked easily…
like they expected the rest of the day
to be good or get better…like radio
announcers for afternoon baseball.
Indiana's muse is an Amish-like August Midwesterner,
his summer straw
an angle and panache
worn geometric to the sun
with thoughts of bruderschaft and light.

50

double seven

Improvisation is calibrated
to find the musical truth
in jazz, in poetry
and in accounting
for that love
We never find directly...damn it!
but in "the scenic truth" (David Mamet)

[Writing in Restaurants] by David Mamet

riff for the pontiff (John 23)

It's not that modern jazz
panders to technocracy.
It's failure is rather because
it has presumed
a creative existence within it.

For the human spirit
to transcend technocracy
it must ride back
to acquire proper habitat
for the human soul

The blood of my heart
riffs red hot
and streaming drunk
amongst the snowbanks

Shoulders are for the martyr's cross
but not for mutilation.
Separately, they're splitting toward the heart's
capacity for union
far greater than ourselves
can ever be.

Every season's
storms of sadness
a life to live
and not another death
Mortified, I am…
Is that an answer?

Big Peasant in Peter's shoes
you have expropriated their place,
bless our prayers to expropriate their purse,
If not by prayers
Perhaps by verse.

blue canto

Off, but moving on to perfect pitch…
Our bluesy nights
and patch of days
lay skiff-like
snow imagined in a cold-marred sky
The grid of our being
…comes tenderly
between the beat
a canto
neither down

nor otherwise
is noted . .
riotously,
How moonlit pale
you turned over…toward me…
will keep thee,
in a kind of veil

laced in your lover's memory

an outside bridge

I remember a bridge
near the park in Leningrad

of russet glint
and gloaming light;
present to the sun

and snow light
repose in a dream
of those environs.

An outside bridge
whose key is otherwise
and cries in that key…

'they've hauled the hammer and sickle down'!
A riff whose sentiment
exceeds its distance
from the truth

of timbres not native
to the stock
of my shotgunned
soul in fugue
for other places

the cello and the coyote

There is a cello in the brush
of snow swept Indiana.
It plays against time-hammered tones.
The cello drifts
over against the terrible note
here…at the end of the score
David Baker's stream unflawed.
A coyote looks into it.

Ramadan

Broken wine glass
on the sink…at dawn

Breaks my fast
…for Ramadan.

Nearly light…the snow

sneaks sinister and white
into my pipes…
which freeze
at the u-joint and elbows.

Cold days that break
in ways…that are sound,
and uncomfortably safe from illusions.

Satiety is essential
for the great Illusion
that in some way
We live apart from God.

Allah sweeps away the full belly
and sensual applause
that we may appreciate
what very little is left.

Apart from sustenance
There is nothing substantive.

Without affection from another
in our way; there is no sense of self.
apart from and without creation,
We are not creative.

But,
hungry, horny, hollow creatures
when reliant on the insatiate self.

Come dear Guardian Lord
Sustain us now
and cherish our best intentions.

As more days break
upon dysfunction's sensibility,
false consciousness
deregulates reality.

When all the breakers
in the box are thrown

Quadr, the Night of Power outages
failures still therein…unknown
akin to death's own fastness
Fast…Alone

the empty quarter

Being there,
is the only substance
and respite
from what begins and ends
being alone
in the empty quarter
stretching between solitary
experiences of birth and death
signifying meaning
more than the sum total

of measures taken.
I would ride
bay pacing camels
into it;
being there
for them
and the objects of prayer.
Hallowed be
thy being there
for me.

Indiana Militia

They ride…
and rein in
near to me.
My regiment
of spectral lancers,
mustered between
Kashghar and Baku.

They've hunted with eagles
in Zalanash, and who
have fed on cool melon
in the heat of Kukhara.
Before the proper mess
before the Registan
they pass
though they pass darkly
through cobbled streets in Samarquand.

After prayers
out to Afrasiab
for buzkashi . . .

Buzkashi . . . !
Cerebral paradigm
for neuro-circuitry of thoughts.

Unimpeded
by illusions of order.

silent cavalry

The secret cause,
the silent cavalry
bivouacked in valleys
of the brain
occlude in rim country
they ride…

a template power of sight (our minister's remarks)

The Indiana militia
in my mind is muslim led.
Judaic strong, and Christian bled
Drill instructors in bow ties and camouflage.
Fruit of Islam and hoosier dread.
Ninety courthouses explode,
the doughboy implodes blasphemous church marquees.
Laughter roils from the dark
continent against cute prayers
from full bellies…

Then deep in the hoosier wood
comes our opposition
to your occupation
when hoosiers run
Indianans take cover.

Hazy thinking
lazy stinking
barricades of bigotry
in camp following churches
of cultural decay.
Decay!

Humid-hearted 'know nothings'
cease and desist your dominance
of God's own heartlanded territories.
Your sinuses wheeze
for Jeeeezus.
His Word denies the sleazes.

As enemies of Redemption you'll be fought
in hill and plain until every meadow, forest, and river
is reclaimed from stupid occupation.
Foliage is fair for Indiana
once hoosier-mindedness is expelled
to the dark and bloody ground below.

And I don't mean Kentucky!

Bosnian and Croat volunteers
are balm for our balkanization.
From the stores of Tripoli,
Papal blessed, Imam addressed . .
come to our aid in this against their sickening gyre.
We'll fight them in their coarsetness
and all their corporate nests.
Psychokinetic artillery
will pillory WASP nests.
Blistering . . feminists
against the elimination of their prime excuse.

Drug addiction will dry up
no longer needed anesthesia
for the unnaturalness.
Secular celebratedness will cease
and go home
or go to work!

Leaving our Indiana women
and men to mind their lord's business

the prophet's ennui

Driving old Ninety-nine
driving the San Joaquin
the Prophet's ennui is between

Merced's river and the Stanislaus.
Woundedness
requires modest redress.

Harden not your heart
an ice hook impales
the new moon of my Christian heart and Jewish mind

Driving an Islamically Informed Sky

the muslim brow of Christ

Why do I feel from where the sounds of Christmas
suggest goodwill…
the brow of Christ contemns?…

Forgiveness requires imagination
both less near death
The motion picture doesn't move much anymore
and there is a sense
the lights will soon come on
Leaving us the stark absence
of what once we helped imagine

under the rain altar

"e lo soleills plovil" (Canto IV Ezra Pound)

The rain, like me, is late…
and still managing.
We've outdogged the drought
and kept our cool . . for those August nights
that frame the lush midsummer's foliage.

After the rain…
during the sweetest shower,
or storm shimmering blur
…before all humid antecedents
we've handled it;
while even seas of soybean
swell and roil like riptides
against the forest green.

I drove east on 36 toward friends in the next county
and saw a sign man hit and killed on the road.
His "time blacked out with the rubber" (Canto VIII)
by a sport ute driven by a mother
chewing gum with tattooed cleavage…

Hadn't seen a man killed in traffic since Moscow in 1960
where the cold crowd moved toward the corpse
with a kind of curious dairy cow interest.

As the dead bury the dead
so losses are left
for those who care most about losing.
This shimmering blur is
me and the rain . . .
still managing.

missing the local

"I'm beginning to live in my job."
Exclusively along and through corridors
of what others call a career.

Increasingly encased within its cold-blooded borders,
it coils and pushes through another day.
With reptilian ignorance of exhaustion it blinks
as the hair on my arms turn gray.

Wrapped around my few and former friends
whose bodies are fallen or dead,
becoming bulbs of passing light.
Impatiently, impatiently, our skins are shed.

No matter the sidelong glancing pace.
Danger was never this dangerous.
Giving with faith that civilization remains someplace
as this fast safeness
whose express line
makes too few stops…
…for living.

reformation in the reformation

A pilgrim church, a godly state
Would help objectify the center
For seeking profiles of god beyond ourselves

Until that time we have access
To provisional truths and the government in exile
Within our consciousness

For conscience is a paradise, still not lost
The essential ally
For restoration of the Soul

Soldier of the Reformation (Hus Envy)

Amid life's migration
soldiering for the reformation
deep entry in the stench
of ecclessialy calibrated death

Nippon trooper near the end
of twenty centuries whose
claim has not come through
the jungles of little people's fever
leprechauns against the light
that lights the ledge
of life still born.

Arrested; the flight of geese
gather shot into their breast
and eyes of wounded flight
look toward its nature
and naturally is not enough
where winter stores the word
endured and yearning back
against the ledge
Hus slipped…design?
or conscious rood can find
freedom finally
understood!

Hus is back/ Your fires die out
And geese are free to fly
the ordained course.

invaded glory

My prayers and will become confused
Destiny and delusion grind together through the night
Triumph of the soul may be too great a contradiction
a third reich of identity with too many fronts.

The war could still be lost
Each battle blends
The apocalypse never comes
The crisis never ends.

Mad roosters crow before the light
Each front a frigate with miles of seas uncrossed
Sacred eyes of storms.

To last could be a prayer, a dream
Or selfish gasp for all that time does not allow
Details of struggle seldom grasp
The weight of faith against itself

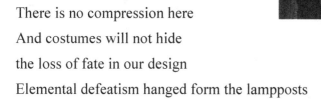

Centrifugal wills tear at the core of things
My powers are gone and comradelessly
The night again recoils
Against the sounds of death

There is no compression here
And costumes will not hide
the loss of fate in our design
Elemental defeatism hanged form the lampposts

Cannot return that strength
We shared when first we conjured holy thoughts to wing
Above the hellish choices of this earth

We chose well and fixed our sights upon the agnus dei
Defiant lamb, God's will to guard, we felt

A risen guide, a chosen, destined way

Greed and the paradise of perspectives lost
Has near mortally hampered
That Purity, which is to will
But one thing

This is not the center of our being
But an offering, forgotten
For dog-soldiered attempts
To save idolatrous appearances

The beauty of God separates from his presence
When value divides from design
The energies accosting fragments of decay
Must be reassembled, and repentant, pay

For centralized defense assured of this one thing
Priorities bride to the only Patriarchal King
All to the Greater Glory of God
Omnia Ad Majorem Gloriam Dei

the deacon

The deacon tends a dark contrast
Away from traffic's plastic light
His night a region of the life

In tones like leaves
That peal
As from a rose at night

the hoary gita

Spaced sociologically
Selves are stars
Forever
In the hoary Gita's breadth

Christ's convergence
Annihilates the personality
That hardest work of prayer
Is to get the Gitas…out

And like the star

"Eat not thy heart", the Sages said;
"nor mourn the Past, the buried Past",
"Do what thou dost, be strong, be brave;
and, like the Star, nor rest nor haste."
                    the Kasidah of
                    Haji Abdu El Yezdi

And, like the star
Mushtari men may see that for our future fall
from whence all ancient light
it falls…

Poles shifting the earth parallel to my forest road
it falls…
distant firework whose sound I cannot hear
it falls…

like the flash of a bad bulb in the front closet
it falls…

And frightens me a bit
like the old buck rabbit who bounded across the road now
it falls…
March slightly crazed and hurtling high into the darkness

And, like the star
I have fallen
mysteriously, mythically, toward
around, into, over, and throughout
all forevers for you
My wife of the Earth
and the heavens

Mother Vi as Visigoth

On to Rome from Terre Haute
the chartered family scene
sped inchoate…,
Me Mother Vi Maureen like Constantine
toured Vatican halls where statues bared their…
walls. And walls around walls, the Cistine
Chapel undulating fleshed tones of color
offended me mother.

"I've seen enough penises in this place
to not have them brandished at Church.
This chapel called Cistine,
to my mind is obscene!
All haunch and grab and reach,
instead of saintly themes,
instead of children
and why Christ bled,"
she said!

A critic blessed,
she then confessed
next door…All
that moral wit; aesthetic call
(within the cathedral) of St. Peter and St. Paul.

sage

divorced between the knife in my boot
and the shoe shine man
the taste of tobacco
and the bloodline numbly feeling

a haircut in the cold night air …
port of kansas city … I unspringingly
rend my steps into your plain
garment of gathering promise

Californians walk into a corner of your sage
waving like the color of a good wife's haunches
show me Missouri, your signs
saving back the break of day

winging jaggedly it flies before me

barely missing barbed wire

another dove feigns injured flight

parental performance more imagined than real

my spaniel eyes seek to nest in safety

great faith and unfeigned flight

increasing part for the Father

to gather promised light.

you're in my light

Light is in and on
the dark of the Wabash
Immanently part...
of what it is not
Ubiquitous it prowls...above
beside and beneath the river
Hunters' moon night sheen
Recall your promise
Pale...and riverine

outlasting

There is a massive eyelet in the west
moving northeast and opening
through grey skies
a light toward yonder space
a window to the soul of heaven
a God's eyedea of soulful yearning
The cloudbank breaks up in the east
betraying else than the skies grey hue
Great cover for the idea
of nothing but ideas
of lone facts that outlast us.

a heart's tack

Gunstocks, saddle, and tack
red and white bird dog, terrier, hound and bay hunter

are the colors that crave
fasthold hope and yearning
for dignity
within my heraldry of seasons

nadryv (Dostoyevskyian)

Absence of the veil
crowd days into close chapters
that lean in the open window
cool to saving appearances
it seals the very book of protection
with a dreadful patientness

Most country music is contrived
to drive night out of the cabin
I love the night
and invite her home.
Slowly now
Sanctify it…

And the tossed black curls
of a catholic child
whose unknown legs
wrap around the fog

her spring-grown hips asunder
St. Anthony's perpetrated steeple
sighing on the great damp lawn of the Asylum

Sidewalk pools reflect
the taste of a screen door
when we all pretended to be kids

Hear crackling hosts in faithful mouths
Fragments of treachery are inadequate
to the import of steadfast refusal

Cast down all images
around the cocktail hour that fail
to exalt the assurance
of that first communion

That "synthesis between culture and faith" (Pope John Paul II)
Clears out the stench of selfies
Dug in like dead mice under the carpet
of our mind.

Falco and Huntzeger's impression management[24]
Cloying crapola
Of craven intentions.

Pubic hair calligraphy
Upon the lip
Of airplane urinals.

Skywriting swollenness
Of the souls incursive avoidance of its source.

How high…
must they fly
to avoid His depth?

[24]Burt Lancaster's 1957 film "The Sweet Smell of Success" revealing the now epidemic infection of unscrupulous counterfeit communication.

Heat upon temples
crave the cold
barrel of a gun
The raging sigh
Of eager fire
Once more from the top. Remember J2P2'
"The synthesis between culture and faith
is not just a demand of culture
but also of faith."

covered bridge

Ride across at a walk
and come out on the inside
of each others mind
at opposite portals
of the bridge covered thought
a few hundred feet in single span
a double seamed burr arch of broken sequences
Dismount to know .. to feel
to enter into and come forth from places
serene…and surreal

[Short Break]

"…of physical and of moral causes and effects ..
we might say the physical are no more than the wooden handle,
whilst the moral are the noble metal, the real bright polished weapon."
Karl von Clausewitz, "Theory of The Art of War"

cold war (bop)

In accordance with section 1084
of the fiscal year 1998 National Defense
Authorization Act, the Secretary of
Defense approved awarding
COLD WAR RECOGNITION CERTIFICATES
to personnel who faithfully and honorably
fought the cold war from (It doesn't say which side!)
September 2, 1945 to December 26, 1991
(I've ordered several)
We didn't start it
and we didn't finish it.
but we sure made it interesting for awhile.

Veterans now pray with the chapped hands

of Muslims in winter

No less deliberate the meander

than avoidant of certain shore lines

Their streams of thought

still elude

ox-bowed illusions of order

open threat to the powers that be

       ("Perhaps the Almighty is also a Trotskyite")

                Isaac Bashevis Singer

Thunder does not carry

its sound bent upward

by waves of warm air

Like thunder, we seem remote to you

an obscure rumbler

in the distant skies

But

we are! Where

you are!

After all the flash and rumble

We will strike you where you live.

fading coal

Once within a showery spring
cold stream sloughing into May
clear rivulet across the valley
pastures feet get wet
Siberian cold to the boot
but champagne to the common soul
that slumped inside of me
cigarette ash red the rose tree
tempt the gasp of trumpets
in my cranium
targets and tiredness
disdain the truth of ancient wisdom
Having fallen in those fields before
for causes greater than I fool myself about

snow lightning

I'd seen a few electrical storms in February
but never as now in the snows of January,
with thunder coming faster that the thaw.
Shaking icicles free from the guttering;
ice breakers of thunder rumbling
behind flashes
of lightning over the snow.

Sluice of May

(Gwalchmar becomes Gwalchaved)
The Sluice of May
into June rain ...
is sliced ...
'As good as rain' ... they say
Tulip poplars blossom
the last of the rite
toward the slower aspect
that stretches out like a child's country road
and lays gentle as a dark warm night
covers for recollection of the hunt
and homecoming thought;
lovemaking the light
come on time

departure from the basic form

Flat head thirds come along seven
Twelve bar blues
We choose…the bluesy weather

démarche

Regions of interiority
began in borders before I was begat
before He knew me in my mother's womb
marchescent but unforsaken
border country between barbarian faith
and Roman Comfort in gaited step
with imagined troops advancing
the cause to go, using force
where only force will do
to steal a march on
clever survival from the others advantage

The march of time…on this land
near these borders steals a march
to gain marchescence with mnemosyne
in the marches of my mind
bordered between my celtic consciousness
and the enemy language…less imposed
than appropriated for raids
on the unspeakable…metaphorsed
upon the dangers of our time
that God has boundaried from eternity
Americain and Trotskyist irrelevance
to the empiricism of empire and capital
without industrial envy
In native foliage
and paraboloid exhaustion
hung over with rusting armor
and Templar responses
to the Arabian daze

Far from the capital of capitols

hinterlanded redoubt

between patriotic gore and the stench of fratricide

I keep my powder dry and await the ages

like a stockdog's "grace of conscious non-assault"

restraint and resistance to the lemmings rush

poetically dwelling in these territories

with mnemosyne…metaphorsed

again and again…t'was ever thus the same

points east of Poland, north of Damascus

or by the Irish Sea near Welsh valleys

on the sunny side of the dark and bloody ground where

Indiana's upriver angels

cause Islamic cocks to crow

throughout the time and shadows

witnessed by the greatest stand of inland trees

grown strong as guards by the aquafir

A sense of safety in these places isolated from the

mainstreams contaminants

Like Morelos above their swamp

Dunlaoghaire from the court

the great San Joaquin

from the cities sloth and the Sierra's vertical brush

the markets of Abergavenny

from Hess's dream of easy peace

"You've come so far," she said in Rhyader

remote as the old mused

on the Cobb and Morgan horses

in cymric grieved the loss

of anyone to Chicago, preferring the plaid

the plaid cymru poetically blowing up

street signs that claimed the lemmings direction

brave Balkans who expelled the turk

after taking his book

against the greater Serbian infection

the nationalist rigor like the map of a California razor

cuts into as well as out of natural law

"We have democracy where we should have liberty

and liberty where we should have democracy", (Hans Morganthau)

the old fencer said, his saber scar

sealed upon his brow like the map of California above teutonic

eyes parrying a career paid for by

powerful enterprise

The purest revolutionary idea

distilled from the old man's death

in Cayoacan to speak Quechuan

with Hugo Blanco and newspeak

with the one-armed man who dragged it

back to town to sleep in lofts with acned ladies

completely capturing himself

and expelling his world to hell

as the best hearts of my generation

they fell…without the dignity

of combative dying … becoming old conversations

that stayed in the city wherein

a zoo of obsolescents they end

without confessional or intercessory prayer

Like coyotes from the Bronx
found in Central Park this season
Natural history reports an unprecedented one thousand
coyote attacks on humans this last year of the century
Indiana's Dept. of Fish and Game report
"brush wolves" or "coyotes" now weighing 70 pounds or more
envoys of nature are convening
protests against the century's violation of natural law.
The Talmud has warned
"Beware of a people ruled
by women and children"
worse if they're genderified
and teenaged on each other
with such unnatural appetites and diet
we only notice when they erupt
into school massacres
and gag the world-wide web
bulemically regurgitating pap
with universal avoidance of the obvious truth

Che died in the marches

of Bolivian obscurity

…Beloved Argentine Mick Cuban Revolutionary

slain by underling

new world authors

of the global underclass

written with tattoos on tits,

ankles and bulging ass

lumpen primaries extend

the white tracks right up their yuppie noses

burning backyard leaves

with black neighbors in North Indianapolis

I heard him fall…

in all…the tearsome Octobers

as our eyes grew sore in smoke

burning leaves from the trefoil, poplar, and green oak

I walked to the fairgrounds with fodder for the horses,

for the song of horses I heard in hoofbeats

down the backstretch and along the tree line toward the tower

of St. Joan of Arc — glimpsed from —

west of the track, above the trees, rail

pounding haunches and urine-stained tail

The sulky's brashness engaged the very air

and soothed the sting in my sight

as Ben Hur's chariot healed Lou Wallace

in his loss of argument to Ingersoll

a story of the Christ that ends with a horse race

bested his speech from Shadowgait's porch

recruiting his regiment against the Confederates

Monocracy of Shiloh

Islam for Billy Bonham

self-recruited Indianan; no Hoosier

Maj. Gen. Lou Wallace was moving toward Debs with Jimmy Riley

The Confederates kept flags in Natchez

We deserve a red American trace

so Lady physicists from Azerbaijan could find themselves

instead of looking for the true American

one block from Dreiser's house.

She complained the Soviets denied her local poets
and made them read Tolstoy, Pushkin, and Dostoyevsky.
My! What suffering … However she always
yearned for Americana and read all of Teddy Dreiser.
Shocked by me she refused to believe
he was as red as Mayakovsky.
What awe-filled sins avenge the Wabash Valley
Treachery unspoken, Bill Harvey comes from Terre Haute Wiley
bonding reaction unbroken at the Central Agency
whose secular fundamentalists hegemaniacally
repress, deceive, destroy, then help, ruthlessly help
to the greatest fragmentation, then call it freedom.

Resistance to slavery, racism, fascism, arrogance, and war
… or the Iron Curtain is easy
compared to the Resistance required
against the new world order of Corporate Timocracy DCLXVI
DOMITIANUS CORPORATUS GEGATOS XTI VILTIER INTERFECIT
The alien slouch of this beast displaces consciousness
from Moscow to Manhattan computing shifty categories
helping every being to be freely non-codependent

from the other, parent, kin, or friend, and all God-consciousness

helping even peripheral places shed traditional theocratic collective values

for their modern marketplace …

"where the seller provides cash for buyers,

devaluing forever their means to close the wound loan" (Prof. Ould Mey)

open threat to the powers that be (Play it agian...Sam!)

("Perhaps the Almighty is also a Trotskyite")

Isaac Bashevis Singer

Thunder does not carry

its sound bent upward

by waves of warm air

Like thunder, we seem remote to you

an obscure rumbler

in the distant skies

But, I am

where you are!

After all the flash and rumble

we will strike you

where you live.

graven genders

Cossack proud, forever humble

They were the yeomen of the valleys

Now downed, unhorsed

To live with female graves

That reek of peasants sleeping

There are dead mice

Under the carpets of their mind

The larval present

Depleting yoemanries hereafter

Good Luck or bad, depends upon the women

And their wombs become like shallow graves

A solar tilt

    From envy

Departure from the woods

A premise for delivery from the Sourceperson

New god for graven genders

Perverted Paraclete, the evil of banality

Pederasts of the backward moving mirror

Someday, Susan B.M. will surely rape her fem

No room now left for stupid optimism

Since Sister Nora slammed that bloody door

Nor quarter for the chronic doomsday crap

None will daunt my spirits
To grab right hold
Where mankind lost his saddle
And ride,
    By Christ,
        I'll ride

time steppe

Heat in August
and a green bottle fly
wake me at midnight;
fanned chapels
cross with Baptist perplextion
scolding the summer's ray
in the dead green eyes of my grandmother's
Indiana.
Blind with August hatreds
she loved me like her Daddy rode down

deserters and cussed the copperheads
though wooed
by a bastard son from Morgan's Cavalry.
In the union of labor and poetry
the Great War of the Rebellion
near suffocates my soul
I sweat upon the scaffolding of thought
and see dust defying time into more dust
along cattle trails in East Africa; maybe a millenium
before the raid at Cooley and taste
blood drawn from the neck of my favorite cow
Horse-kicked and hot in the caucuses
trying to keep flies off my wounds
ordained for war in the delirium of Peace…
I can't find my helmet!

errant night

The last errant night of this century
which began in the stench
of the trench
in the not so silent night
of consciousness exceeding christendom
ends now, not in repose…now active
interior curias and caliphates will recall
all the tragic losses…as so much
white boys' angst.
Lack of hope is not lack of vision
no more than necessity is a virtue
hubris …hubris…
whether pagan, providential, or socialist
external certitude is but a trusted guide
against ambivalence,
idolatrous only when believed i.e., deceived
the white bull carries off our daughter.

Five thousand years from the shores of Crete
and we're only left with the Amish
ideas of civilization more dangerous
than the naturally improved reality we respect
paying homage to Nature
as Priest of the Trees
Faith is not certainty
but the courage
to navigate
uncertainties.

floodmarks

- her darkest eyes and palest flesh
does not dissuade; does not dispel
that madness, akin to passion
more falsely conscious than death in hell
- it sweeps vast meadows of our mind
a grim and jagged scything, yet it floods
over sluice of soul and conscious lock it comes

in spate, and injured seiche it floods
- no clinical windlass, no prayerful shade
levers against its rise
and terrible blood now settles
in our eyes

synecdochical

I attended Universities
from vodka lit fires
ash diamonded in cadre trained terror
toward leisure's of the theory class
Discordant as the blind piano tuner
transposed the time
from Union Grand to winter's air
where the lab dogs howled
above Meyers Hall near the sound of cellos
Seeking contradictions of escape and connection
like the dogs' yearning
for a human touch, a sovereign hand
even if it held

a knife or ether cone

Things first; becoming ideas

etherized by fact

What's the matter?!

for the things made of it;

a walking synecdoche ... nearly schizoid in detail

discalculiated and swept into the mural

time loses it's grammar points

in deserts empty ground

lightning strikes you

cause nothing else's around

hardlight

In Indiana, you can enjoy spring all summer

if you get up early enough for it

After dawn, you begin to feel the heat behind

the cool of morning, like the hot, dry muzzle

of a sick hound

Indiana at points is greener than Ireland

Humid cool, damp, cold, or scalding

Its haze of humidity precedes the sun

in this world; conserving the ancient

mist and cloud of those awe filled regions

before the hard light

limberlost idea

The grey heron rose …

an ungainly polemic

against cement

Cutting down clouds

Her argument

deep in the evening skies

quotation of queen Anne's lace

swam in the air

like a young cow in water

animysteriad

I rarely run over creatures
The few times I've struck a beast,
heard the thump of steel or rubber
bump and crush fur and flesh
glimpsed the flat or twisting death
in my mirrors
it has become a very bad time
An omen of money, weather or love going bad
A kind of divine-like disapproval
of what I'd done and become
The native mind knew
we'd come to naught
dying alone after wasting time
… and the natural good
Running over things,
wasting life with the loss
of graced moments with wild creatures

who hallowed be, do not strive to become
God's eyes who close on the periphery
of wherever we're going
as we run over them
Tecumseh knew our last abode
and smiled into significant stasis
a preordained pivot, Tecumseh died in Canada
Tecumseh's brother knew
after blarneying the government bullets
dying peacefully in Kansas, I think the Prophet knew

she is my chardonay

Roaring lambs of March
begin to bleat and alter the thaw
of fickle warmth
with the wind so full of winter
we waited where
the air was spring-broken
and our hearts grew harder there

May light lasts

through the shadows of summer

bordered along roads I'd discover

drawing the idea of her

from whole seasons in a day

strangelight drawn desirably

soft in the afternoons

heat advisories for the healing light

Subtly golden-hearted

the color of sin in contexts

she is moral Chardonay

interpenetrating my falleness; turning it away

comely while leaving

Aye, the burnished wood!

Taupe and maroon as tannin

a wine dark wood in this light

which is the last light

of an early winter's day

caressing so long

comely while leaving

Sure, and it's more

than fires on the sun

weathered obligation

There were signs of clear and present danger

Until the weather changed

Hell's wasting oven

Gentled by the climate of salvation

Both hushed and wakened by the rain

From voyeuristically hung open-eyed floating

Unlidded labias of insignificant consumption

That consume and soothe

The world's regurgitated imitation

Of Foster Selves, that cannot tell

The content of themselves

The undernourished gluttony of social intercourse

And the foundering of innocents

Makes lies a lice

That sucks the strength from Obligation

Simone Weil's Obligation, and mine, and thine

To hallowed be

And quench tapers for the Foster Self

Wasted evening,

    Rain freshened aim

september skies

The red wines of september skies

drives one inside

for evening pleasure

tannin promise

of comfort from the coming cold

the hidden sea

"Our daily thought was certainly but the line of foam at the edge of a vast and
luminous sea"

W.B Yeats

<u>Anima Hominus</u>

"Your limbs shall Spirit be

You'll see the deep deep land"

Karl Marx

<u>Siren Song</u>

The Kildeer are gulls of the valley

Arcing up away and back upon the land

Searching for the sea beneath the ground

The air and breath of Vaughn white mornings on the fragipan

Raging still below the land-locked beach

Lost rivers flow and fastly calm

The hidden sea,

The buried vast and varied main

Exists to purge our mortal natures
Naumachian legions of the deep contain
Sea fighting rivers
Pouring in upon our brain

The inland flood recounters consciousness
Charybdis within her heavy hair
Strange swimmer, for walking on these waters underground
You've scared Sycllan flight again

"I would rather be feared than loved
For growing power upon the waters
Except that I love you," became the plea of Glaucous
As he turned mentalities enchantment

Imploring angry heavens to flesh his sword
Away from solitude, and 'slip the dogs of war'
Save them from sleeping in the manger
"Voe victus!" "to your tanks O Israel"

Logomachus words at his command
Imbrued the truth in blood

For that's where truth belongs
Lochabar axe, halberd, and gaft – a skean for all that's scotched

Type and personification, shadow upon shadow
Inner penetrate the mind
Dominus dialecticum
Of Them and us and Him

Our youth unslaked and planet struck
He swam the whale path drowning
A Jonahed, lascar, jacky
Oarsmen for the red sea battery

Lord God of Whales who sing of sins and weep
Cauldrons of fiery blood
Who boil beneath the surface of the deep

Assist seaworthiness
Oppose mosaic violence
That placed her breast against the wave
In beastly form she chose to thrash against the coping stones

Between eros and agape
Stars of David stumbled in
Upon the nun
Of Celibacy's prairie

"The waves were not like water
They were like falling city walls"
"Rosa alchemical," "unreckonable wandering"
Near the plain of Sharon

We are but the trembling
Of this great wave's lips
Monachamous converging
The costal guns are spiked

All the coastal guns are spiked
The lance is couched
Time to close the temple doors
Of January

Love never finds a place
In sharken twisted waters

Prey escapes

To contemplate the sun

Upon a buoy's attempted glimpse of light

Bright bell alone, above less darkened sharkened waters

Secured to care in depths where it is stillest

Their love endures the Hidden Sea

bottom land

I have yearned and I have grieved

through darknesses

that occlude my heart.

Where light is shorn from life

When end shear… insures

the taste…of gloom.

scimitar

The first chill of that last year
in cold northern towns was scimitar light slanting
from ear to ear of our dreams
Defeat in Burgos
tasted like a stone axe

shadows at noon

    (or the gloom of Zephaniah)
The darkening came in May;
colors of the deer and rabbit
staying everywhere except on the grass.
Great swards of grass
yet dimly reflect the pastures of heaven
when the sky remains a grand cavern
tunneling out from winter
with little spring light at the end of it.
Hope can wilt in such weather
like an incarcerated dream

with dwindling income,

hysteria showers about and hides in the shadows at noon.

This sick and unseasonable shade

can arrest love's bloom

unless to act with such purity of will

we rend all heartlessness

by racing criminally fast

into the rainbow.

beyond the pale

"Wildered and dark" (Coleridge) in the time it takes your watch

    to stop

While a woods cat

can break in your screen,

raid the kitchen

and scare the shit

out of your house cat

You may wonder

whether it is bravery

or the brute
in you that yearns
for that wild
in the bison's eye
Large-lashed and luminous
a massive pool
of dark consciousness
which hates my paleness
across the fence
Ancestral trace from this ancient breed

explanatory weather

Shut up, it explained
and won't let go
of the morning
making evening
a gentler surprise

ballad from a still pond

A harmonic moment
has to do with the waters
turning over in the universe.
Clear moments upon the surface
of a season changed
Perpendicular to the sun-shot
arc of the vernal equinox
lay undulating
beneath what's up
in the thermocline
Prescient still
pond,
and lake potion
not fanfared
nor vulgar
but still

hail the grief

(…a beaten dog beneath the hail) Ezra Pound Canto 99)

Light is present

in the March green rain

under the tumult of old skies

the new scene disguise

is hailed, boarded

nailed, and bordered

severely, sincerely

cold and wise

weather that soulfully

falls with the ice

the fall of light

In late summer

the Hoosier morn

so usually hot

comes suddenly cool,

soothing the melon workers

in their August sweat
and kills off the tick season;
an iced liniment
for the old season's weather
more explanatory weather
Shut up!, it explains
to all litigants of humidity
bringing even the doves
off the ground
where just this side of resignation
sad they sound
marginal to the wind
and any old weather
it sounds the trace
of ancient longing
To be …no
from where we've seen
to be where…
we ought to've been.

impermanent pasture

(Not even the seasons
are as permanent
as our ideas about them)
There are new colors
darker, deeper, dawner
not darkened at noon
but nooner – eveninger
a gloaming coverlet
for the catholic day
a bold black and white print
from the front –
rotagravured –
brown-sectioned bright
beyond technicolors
when the night's
southwestern air borne highly
loud around us;

that 'certain' 'unnamable' light

not 'slant'ed nor november any more like the light seems

an ablated remnant

and endpiece as yet unsold.

'Ill seen' and unsaid as cornstalks

fall...celebrating their harvest

in epilogues of colder light

...the senses swirl

chiefly...around native springs

through covered bridges worn

as well as willed to gird

her perihelion;

this century's ending night

this perigee;

This closing light.

keep from falling

       "blossoms of the Apricot

       blow from the east to the west

       and I have tried to keep them from falling"

                        Canto XIII

                        Ezra Pound

Il Purgatorio past Patterson's intensities solo,

kept fast on the west side of War and Peace.

Intensities between Yosemite and the sea,

intensities that are hard light;

glintsome against an armour

lit across the Valley's floor.

Not stumbling, nor at march

I keep from falling

simply by recall …

astride the fast, hard light.

No blossoms, but a focused laser

upon the western night.

April was cruel no longer

As I walked to work without a coat
The air was cool as her hand
touching old fevers
We settled into the returning season
Resilient as the breeze

one night away

The nine o'clock night colors green
in my headlights against the trees
near, and surrounded by the darkest shade
is fate the sovereign's kept forever
One night away.

lakes of grass

I concelebrate consciousness
non assumptem est
collective and decoupling
I presume the rest

emits atomic light
beyond the earthbound self
There are Seas of grass
flowing west of the Wabash
unto the Pacific
There are Leaves of grass
in leys east of the Ohio
unto the Atlantic
But, O my lakes of grass
are here
in the broken heartedland
where green weeds sprout
from the prayers of Pascal
in the ruin of failing factories
in swards so green … They're blue
(Distant galaxies blue)
Lespideza, Rye
Orchard, Timothy
and Tall Fescue

Whole lakes of grass
the deepest hue
so green
that seen
in returning flights
from Ireland
even then
the experience of Emerald
is deepened:
Have I mentioned Clover!
Red or white
sheep or sweet
in leys
for the lakes of grass

Not for the way
they have gone
but forever and a day
My lakes of Grass
WILL STAY.

not an albatross

Picture a seagull on the Wabash
thousands of miles from the sea.
The sight of a lone gray gull
on this wintry inland waterway.)

Such a one was seen on New Year's Day,
wheeling by ice flows on the Wabash;
white and gray as the river's question
mark against the burnished wood.

I parked off the bridge, my nerves ...
meandering – through the morning haze
to accompany the flight and ways
of nature's otherwise expectation
that gulls should be away in some other place.

In some dumb subtropical splendor or near Northern Seas,
not problematically here and solitary.
Cold suspect, are you lost or vaguely free
to haunt this unappreciated – riverine

heartland of dark contradictions?

The seagull on the Wabash did not respond to me!
distance is not his problem, I believe
but the depth and fortune of seasonally
changing dramas. Similarly, yet
strange. It is akin to our ancient responsibility
passed into climes beyond expectations
to neither value nor respond to surprise.
Into times that are new for the ancient ability
to respond like the gull on the river
        ...to be otherwise.

rotars

The spring hatch of reptiles
fill the frog pond full of sound
castanets that rotar a spacecraft
away from earth and mortality

Rotary sounding cymbals
knawing alone at the edge of it
quaking partitions
of consciousness

Pushing off – shipping out
from the veil of appearances
remotely withdrawing
as time turns out the baby frog in the bass's belly

There is no pleasure in…insignificance
or significance for that matter…eliminative
of circumstance, material witness
to the bass's head I nail to the wall

No Gnats in Goshen*

(or Ode to Drosophilia)

[Allah disdains not to use
the similitude of things,
even of a gnat. S.2A26
The Holy Koran]

They were at the wedding
old comrades I'd studied in '60
swarming about the mimosa
and around the old groom's head;
genetic pilots and precursors of wrath.
I had not met that hope
of her father, the bride's father
we buried two winters ago,
drilling the frozen earth with machinery
for his grave and our prayerful loss
in a cold hard hole.
Taps touched his daughter's tears
and tore off past fallen graves
away from the mine ground and over
the rolling land his life had loved
worked and welded
into the flesh of evening.

* Goshen: Eastern district of the Nile delta.
Fertile land Joseph gave his brothers.

134

They're around the brideshead now;

the cloud upon the veil

led by the cyclic ampresponsive

element binding protein

through 30 day life cycles

since I was in school

and knew their 480th predecessors.

Insect intelligence like a forty-year old man

remembering one hell of a shock at twelve.

Harrowing home-centered hope …

his cousins rabbits could have seen

from their upland hutch

triangulated to the point of her murdered husband,

our grandfather's grey countenance

drawing the line in winter fields deflecting one,

and accepting another into the ground

of our being as more than old snow

transmitted clear by his cyclic ampresponsiveness …

elemental as the clean wood

on his radio.

His issue dying now … near evening

also far … in the city of angels

going to Mass in Spanish

since they changed it from the latin

preferring aesthetic non communication

to infantile patter

particles of labrynthian infrastructure

driving the megapolis model

of life without centers

I longed for my father's bar

where they could still translate gemuchlekeit

and dream of gemeinschaft

I feared the bulbous fracture gimme – gimme

mein schaft bent over and rapacious gezellschaft

degenerately peddled by heirs of puritans

in pervasive propaganda.

The goldfinch in showery rain

gripping a green branch

of the berry tree

is submerged in the summer shower

and bright presence

of the sun's promise

to shower tomorrow.

As time goes by for the goldfinch

my father's fathers enjoyed this wild canary.

If we are the entire cast

of our Freudian dreams.

Why aren't we the all

of the waking dream of consciousness,

the bird, branch, and gnats

of our ancestors ampresponsiveness.

"Dark time haunts us with the briefness of our days."

Thomas Wolfe
'Of Time and the River'

"…and I am waiting happily
for things to get much worse
before they improve…"

Lawrence Ferlinghetti, 1960
Waiting for the Rebirth of Wonder

"…and I am waiting in wonder
for things to get even better
before they fall apart…"

Thomas Morgan, 2000
Watching the Stillbirth of Times Sad Measure

"Time…is so everything doesn't happen at once."

Albert Einstein
On Relativity

Only the River "But for the River,…big and powerful . . the only natural force that can wholly determine the course of human peregrination."

T.S. Eliot (From an Introduction to Huck Finn)

(In the near future and not so distant past…)   [Brief Set]

There is a ring-eyed bulldog
    in my verse
dozing like the history
Of my people's memory
Wastefully distracted by bitches in heat
And no home training
At times he bites
    the wrong people
And has killed some poems
Between his teeth, leaving
The metres bleeding

He's not the dog he's meant to be
Bloodlines are bordered only by the imagination
And his jaws are locked on a dreams refrain.
"It was the last thing he'd written", the Captain
said. And then handed us the Covington paper.
A back page read,
"Cossack of the Valley is Dead."

The three of us had been called here aboard the Riverboat where he'd died. Monsignor Finn, Jack Fields and me. My name is Isaacs.

Somebody said, "Davies was a man of the valleys."
Fields smirked.
"Davies was a man who lived, thought, and wrote in fragments. You called it poetry. I call it disorganization."

"Well, that must be why you're in on the will, Jack . . he figured we all needed a good organizer."

"Cute!" Fields said and walked away toward the ship's bar. And be damned if we didn't follow him. Fields was like that, even when you disliked him you ended up following him. A born leader, that was Fields. He always reminded me of the Lorenz theory of leadership. That is, if you take an individual sheep from a leaderless flock and lobotomize it, removing all traces of flock instinct it will without any regard for others go its own way with all the others following it. And like that, all of us sheep followed that self-centered son-of-a-bitch up to the bar.

I disliked him more when I saw he'd ordered a bloody mary and was worrying over the long piece of celery stuck in it. I even began to feel a little superior by ordering Brown and branch water, the way old Davies used to.

The bar itself was magnificent. It ran the length of the starboard hall and gleamed like a gunstock. I was settling in to just enjoy looking at it and lazily studying its grain when Fields grabbed hold of our minds and made us get to business.

"We can liquidate this property by Friday and I'll be taking the first weekend plane I can get from Cincinnati back to New York."

"We'll be down river by then."

"You'll be down river . . I'll be in Cincinnati,"

"The will says…"

"What it says is not binding. Is it, counselor?"

His lawyer had joined us.

"No, sir'h, no court in Kaintuckiano would hold you to it."

Batman's "the joker" with a bourbon accent was this lawyer. The scion of decadence Fields used to call him. Apparently the group in New York still used him in midwestern cases, for here he was fluttering around Fields like a fruit fly. I began to bait him for having lost yet another wife and how I thought lawyers were carnally inadequate. I could tell Fields liked to see him picked on so I laid it on pretty hard. After a few minutes he slunk off to a table with the captain and the priest.

Fields motioned to a table near the end of the bar and we sat down with our drinks there. He had co-opted the spirit of things quick enough and was drinking Brown and water himself now.

"What's with you, Rolphe," he asked me, twisting his chin sideways. We used to joke about how Fields always seemed to be talking out the other side of his mouth.
    "You need a vacation from the Oakland Soviet?"

It was going to be political. Two coast factionalism in the middle of America with Will Davies not even in the ground yet. I didn't want it to be political, not now.

"The trip's paid for and it's what the old man wanted," I said, "you afraid to spend three more days with real Communists?"

"You!", he laughed. "I spend hours every day with hundreds like you. It's the priest and the time to say nothing of the corpse that I object to." I'd never been able to get to Fields, but Will Davies had. In fact, Will was probably the only man living or dead who'd been able to get to him. I looked at him closely and said, "He always spoke well of you, Jack."

We continued to drink the rest of the afternoon. After all, the will provided for bar bill, meals and passage for the three executors from the Cincinnati-Covington locks down the Ohio, past Louisville to Newburg, then up the Wabash to Terre Haute for the funeral. The Covington newspaper had really carried on about this last leg of the trip. It seems Will Davies had something to do with getting the Wabash opened up again for rivercraft. High school bands which he hated and the "Valley's Labor Councils" which he loved were going to greet us "on the banks of the Wabash and carry their native poet, their fallen comrade, home to his final resting place." The article went on and on, sappy but salutary. It quoted an I.S.U. professor as saying, "He was one of Terre Haute's great radical sons in the tradition of Theodore Dreiser and Eugene Debs." Will sure had a friend on that Covington paper.

For a long while, Fields and I went round and round like two tomcats with their tails in the air. Using Havana cigars like shortswords, to poke at each other while we argued. Those cigars were, I think, the best part of the will. The first couple of hours we ritually touched on our factional disputes, traded horror stories, and scandals, accusing his people and then mine of being a disgrace to the movement. We began to toast each other after a particularly good insult, and the waiter would come like an inevitable footnote at the end of some rabbinical bullshit asking, "More Brown and branch water, gentlemen?" And Fields would answer back, "Yeah, but not too much branch water." So, after a two-hour glow of Brown and not too much branch water, Fields' mind ceased to whir like a Machiavellian engine and a kind of comradely stupor settled in.

He began to resemble the left wing amputee I'd first met him as back in college. An embittered cripple the opposition taunted at a picket line. That was the first time I saw Fields go for the eyes. He would not tolerate remarks about the stump, which was cut and healed about 3 inches back from the wrist on his left arm. But otherwise he was all wit and brilliance. It had been a pleasure to be with him in those days. He'd been to Cuba on a Fulbright in 1960 and actually spoken to the bearded saints we could only eulogize. He said he joined the movement when he finally met folks he couldn't out argue, that is, not without lying. When he couldn't lie any longer he joined up in Chicago, went to leadership school and was sent to minister to us in the provinces.

Suddenly, someone was saying, "And here is the main attraction of your inheritance property, gentlemen." We both looked through the blur of altogether too much J.T.S. Brown to see the captain standing squarely there and holding something. He'd left the barroom and come back with…"What the hell has he got there?" Fields was asking and kicking me under the table. The captain stood like a block, his short arms in a brass-buttoned blazer holding something.

"What the hell is he holding?" Fields really landed one to my shins. It was a black and white pit bull.

"Captain Stone is holding, my good man, the ring-eyed bulldog escaped from his verse."

"What?"

"It's "Will Davies' pit bulldog, sir. Apparently the three of you have inherited it."

aphelion (portrait of the artist on and as an olde horse)

I ride the October night
obtuse; as a skeleton might
Night-sprinted like
an abstract being
I ride partial phases
of the moon; white
as a bone and
ribcaged above
the earth I'm bound
to spasms of pain
since the slime of my birth.
Soulforce rides
through the visceral
delusions of heaven
not unclothing life
from time unto eternity

Time is the school in which we learn...

The Saints: Terre Haute Swing Band, 1953

Time is the fire in which we burn.
— Delmore Schwartz

Portrait of the Artist on and as an old horse

The Music has come a long way since its beginning in the late 19th century. However, the overall climate in the United States in this early 21st century—a surging White supremacy, an unleashed capitalist class, a weakened labor movement—indicates that…the path ahead will continue to be rocky indeed.

Gerald Horne

Jazz & Justice

Destruction of Time: Bibliography

Hudson, Richard. "Stolen Time": The History of Tempo Rubato Clarendon Press, Oxford 1994

Horne, Gerald " Jazz & Justice: Racism & the political Economy of Music" NYU Press 2019

Griffin, Farah J. & Salem Washington. "Clawing at the limits of Cool" Thomas Dunne Books 2008

Marable, Manning. "Malcolm X" Penguin Books 2011

Matejka, Adrian. "The Big Smoke" Penguin Books 2013

McGeachy, M.G. "Lonesome Words: Vocal poetics of Old English (Lament & African – American Blues" Palgrave Macmillan 2006)

Ayerton, Pete. "Revolution! Writings From Russia1917" Pegasus Books 2017

Genovese, Eugene D. "Roll Jordan Roll" (The World The Slaves Made) Voltage Books 1976

Reynolds, Roger. "A Searchers Path (A Composers Ways)" ISAM Monographs #25 1987

Whitehead, Colson. "The Underground Railroad" Anchor Books 2018

Wolff, Francis. "The Blue Note Years" (Cuseuna, Lourie, & Schneider) Rizzoli Press 1995

Burrell, David B. "Towards A Jewish – Christian – Muslim Theology" Wiley Blackwell Publication 2011

ACKNOWLEDGEMENTS

Great thanks to my eldest son, Eliot Thomas Aquinas, for the design of photo coordination with jazz and poetry here. And to my dearest daughter, Bethany Kate, for her insight, resources and constant influence. My gratitude also to the friends, family (beloved wife Wendi), comrades and community for their support. I would especially thank Jon Robeson, Director of Arts Illiana, for his encouragement. And for Barbara Barajas whose patient typing transformed my long handed scribbling. It should also be gratefully noted the tone of Warren Barbour's Terre Haute blues trumpet inspired my own…if more in words than brass.

Warren Barbour - Wiley 1949

Warren Barbour (1931-2020) who captured the tone of Terre Haute with his horn; playing throughout the 50's and 60's with all the great jazz men and women of the Wabash Valley; he held forth from The Boat Club, The Dew Drop, The Cabin, The Idaho, The Spot, Little Havana, Hotel Filbeck and The Terre Haute House.

ALSO BY T.G.M

Not of Our Time

Shotgun Preacher

Glimpses

Thomas G. Morgan is available for select speaking engagements.
To inquire about a possible appearance call 765.245.1413

www.ThomasGMorgan.com

> *"Not since Ted Dreiser have we heard from Terre Haute, Indiana, such hard words, tenderness, and commitment of an American writer. Way to go Tom. "*
>

SHOTGUN PREACHER

Where the Cold and Old political wars of the sixties began to converge with the culture wars of this new century

GLIMPSES (MEMOIR)

This life with its glimpses of goodness, is still a terrible probation
THE HOLY KORAN 3/85

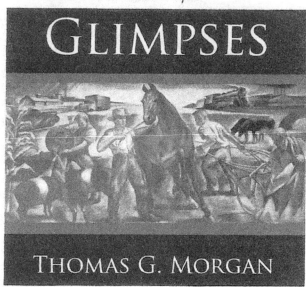

NOT OF OUR TIME

The poet asks that we consider a collective consciousness in a society which celebrates the personality

*Throughout the 60's and 70's Tom Morgan published poetry and essays considered by some to have proven prophetic. In the 80's, his 'Not of Our Time' displayed Vasnetsov's painting 'Warrior at the Crossroads.'
A weary knight and his tired horse stop before an inscribed stone: 'If you go Left, you will lose your horse. If you go right you will lose your head.' Tom has spent a lifetime in ways so as not to lose his horse or his head. Seldom do modern writers take on this range of experienced feeling. His intensity is like that of Jacob wrestling the Angel*

JIM MOORE
CURATOR EMERITUS OF ALBUQUERQUE'S
MUSEUM OF WESTERN ART AND HISTORY.

CPSIA information can be obtained
at www.ICGtesting.com
Printed in the USA
BVHW011209290522
638170BV00006BA/66